OUT
TO PASTURE!

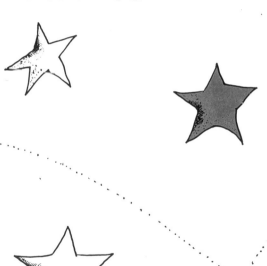

Make Me Laugh!

OUT
TO PASTURE!

jokes about cows

by Joanne E Bernstein & Paul Cohen
pictures by Joan Hanson

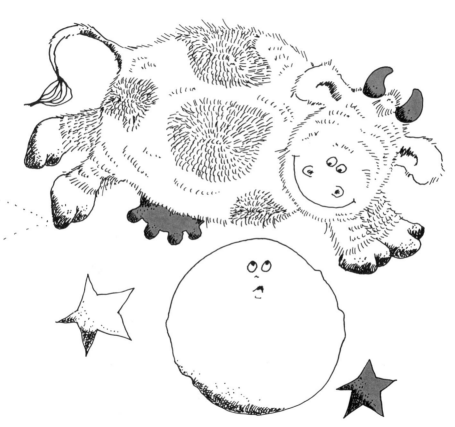

Lerner Publications Company ◆ Minneapolis

To Gila — J.B.
To the students and staff of Lafayette High School,
1966-1986 — P.C.

Library of Congress Cataloging-in-Publication Data

Bernstein, Joanne.
  Out to pasture!

  (Make me laugh!)
  Summary: A collection of jokes about cows, such as
"How do cattle defend themselves? Cow-a-ti."
  1. Cows—Juvenile humor. 2. Wit and humor,
Juvenile. [1. Cows—Wit and humor. 2. Jokes.
3. Riddles] I. Cohen, Paul, 1945-   . II. Hanson,
Joan, ill. III. Title. IV. Series.
PN6231.C24B47   1988   818′.5402   87-22720
ISBN 0-8225-0998-9 (lib. bdg.)

Manufactured in the United States of America

  2   3   4   5   6   7   8   9   10   97   96   95   94   93   92   91   90   89

Q: What do you get when you cross a steer
with a toad?
A: A bullfrog. (Or a horned toad.)

Q: How is a cow like a teddy bear?
A: They're both cud-dly.

Q: What can't the bankrupt cowboy complain?
A: He's got no beef.

Q: What did the cow say when she stepped into the bread?
A: "Hoof a loaf is better than none."

Q: What do you get when you cross a calf with a kitten?

A: Veal catlets.

Q: How does a farmer collect fertilizer?
A: All the cows chip in.

Q: When do you put milk in your ear?
A: When it's past-your-eyes-d (pasteurized).

Q: Where do cows eat lunch?
A: At the calf-eteria.

Q: What do calves eat when they're sick?
A: Chicken moo-dle soup.

Q: What's the best way to keep milk from turning sour?

A: Keep it in the cow.

Q: Are bulls dignified?

A: Yes, they're always cow-teous, and behave in a manner be-hoof-ing the gentleman.

Q: What style of clothing do cows wear?

A: Tail-ored.

Q: What's the difference between a cow and a broken chair?

A: One gives milk, and the other gives way (whey).

Q: Who turned the milk cow into a beautiful princess?

A: Her dairy godmother.

Q: How do you destroy Cow-nt Dracula?
A: Drive a heart through his steak.

Q: In which movie did Dorothy meet the Scare-cow?
A: The Wizard of Ox.

Q: Which television program shows cow oddities?
A: "Bull-ieve It Or Not."

Q: What do you get from Dr. Frankenstein's cow?

A: Monster cheese.

Q: Do cows like riddles?

A: Yes, they find them a-moo-sing. (But oxen like yokes.)

Name three cow nursery rhymes.
"Chew, Chew, Chew Your Cud"
"Three Blind Moos"
"Cheese Porridge Hot"

Q: What animals do you bring to bed?

A: Your calves.

Q: Who delivers little cow babies?
A: The steer-k.

Q: What do you call a cow fad?
A: The latest graze.

Q: Why don't cows smile?
A: Would you smile if your mother gave you grass for dinner every night?

Q: What does a cow do when someone insults her?
A: She goes off in a hoof.

Q: What do you call a cattle hippie?

A: A beef-nik. (Or a member of the cow-nter culture.)

Q: Which cows get into college?
A: Only the cream of the crop.

Q: What happened to the lost cattle?
A: Nobody's herd.

Q: What's the difference between a schoolboy
studying and a farmer watching his cattle?
A: One is stocking his mind, and the other
is minding his stock.

Q: How did the first cows come to America on the Moo-flower?

A: In steerage.

Q: Where do cows like to live?
A: St. Moo-is, Moo-ssouri, and Moo Jersey.

Q: How many cows live on this earth?
A: Bull-ions.

Q: Where do Russian cows live?
A: Moo-scow.

Q: Why doesn't Sweden export cattle?
A: Because they want to keep their Stockholm.

Q: How do cattle defend themselves?
A: They know cow-a-ti.

Q: What must cattle remember to bring to camp?

A: Their cow-meras.

Q: What do cows say when they play hide-and-seek?

A: "Leather or not, here I come."

Q: When does a bull charge?

A: When something Angus him.

Q: What is the bulls' favorite game?
A: Cowhide-and-seek.

Q: What did the cow wear to the football game?

A: A Jersey.

Q: Where do cow football games take place?

A: In the steer-dium.

Q: What is in the middle of the cows' football game?

A: Hoof-time. (Often called calf-time.)

Q: Why do cows run in herds?
A: So they can get their sneakers wholesale.

Q: Which cow baseball player holds the most milk?

A: The pitcher.

Q: If you find cows in the bullpen, where do you find sheep?

A: In the bleat-chers.

Q: What does the umpire say to start the cow baseball game?

A: "Butter up!"

Q: What do cows like best at the gym?
A: The moo-sage.

Q: Where does a cow record daily events?
A: In a dairy.

Q: Why can't you shock cows?
A: They've herd it all.

Q: How do cows spread the news?
A: They send a bull-etin.

Q: Why are cows snitchers?
A: Because they're cattle-tales.

Q: What do you call an Asian ox who talks all the time?

A: A yak-ety-yak.

ABOUT THE AUTHORS

PAUL COHEN AND JOANNE BERNSTEIN are teachers who graze in Brooklyn, New York, in pastures near Cow-ney Island. Paul and his wife Marie enjoy travel, gardening, and music. Paul is also a passionate Mets fan. Joanne, her husband Michael, and calves Robin and Andy enjoy computers, word games, and their summer cow-tage in Maine. Paul and Joanne blow their own horns in saying this is their seventh riddle book together.

ABOUT THE ARTIST

JOAN HANSON lives with her husband and two sons in Afton, Minnesota. Her distinctive, deliberately whimsical pen-and-ink drawings have illustrated more than 30 children's books. Hanson is also an accomplished weaver. A graduate of Carleton College, Hanson enjoys tennis, skiing, sailing, reading, traveling, and walking in the woods surrounding her home.

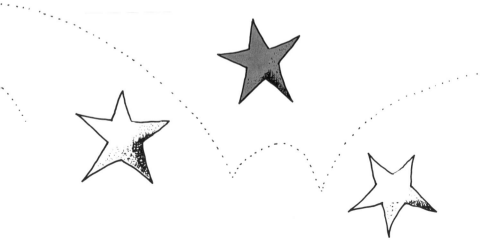

Make Me Laugh!

CAN YOU MATCH THIS?
CAT'S OUT OF THE BAG!
CLOWNING AROUND!
DUMB CLUCKS!
ELEPHANTS NEVER FORGET!
FACE THE MUSIC!
FOSSIL FOLLIES!
GO HOG WILD!
GOING BUGGY!
GRIN AND BEAR IT!
HAIL TO THE CHIEF!
IN THE DOGHOUSE!
KISS A FROG!
LET'S CELEBRATE!
OUT TO LUNCH!

OUT TO PASTURE!
SNAKES ALIVE!
SOMETHING'S FISHY!
SPACE OUT!
STICK OUT YOUR TONGUE!
WHAT A HAM!
WHAT'S YOUR NAME?
WHAT'S YOUR NAME, AGAIN?
101 ANIMAL JOKES
101 FAMILY JOKES
101 KNOCK-KNOCK JOKES
101 MONSTER JOKES
101 SCHOOL JOKES
101 SPORTS JOKES

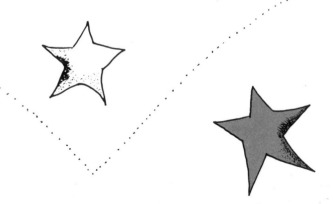